Higher Scores on Math Standardized
Grade 4 Answer Sheet

MW01016271

STUDENT'S NAME		SCHOOL:
LAST	FIRST · MI	TEACHER:

FEMALE ○   MALE ○

BIRTH DATE

MONTH	DAY	YEAR
Jan ○	⓪ ⓪	⓪ ⓪
Feb ○	① ①	① ①
Mar ○	② ②	② ②
Apr ○	③ ③	③ ③
May ○	④	④ ④
Jun ○	⑤	⑤ ⑤
Jul ○	⑥	⑥ ⑥
Aug ○	⑦	⑦ ⑦
Sep ○	⑧	⑧ ⑧
Oct ○	⑨	⑨ ⑨
Nov ○		
Dec ○		

GRADE   ②   ③   ④   ⑤   ⑥

**Higher Scores on Math
Standardized Tests, Grade 4
© Steck-Vaughn Company**

(Name grid columns: A B C D E F G H I J K L M N O P Q R S T U V W X Y Z)

Pretest, part 1

1. Ⓐ Ⓑ Ⓒ Ⓓ   5. Ⓐ Ⓑ Ⓒ Ⓓ   9. Ⓐ Ⓑ Ⓒ Ⓓ   13. Ⓐ Ⓑ Ⓒ Ⓓ   17. Ⓐ Ⓑ Ⓒ Ⓓ
2. Ⓐ Ⓑ Ⓒ Ⓓ   6. Ⓐ Ⓑ Ⓒ Ⓓ   10. Ⓐ Ⓑ Ⓒ Ⓓ   14. Ⓐ Ⓑ Ⓒ Ⓓ   18. Ⓐ Ⓑ Ⓒ Ⓓ
3. Ⓐ Ⓑ Ⓒ Ⓓ   7. Ⓐ Ⓑ Ⓒ Ⓓ   11. Ⓐ Ⓑ Ⓒ Ⓓ   15. Ⓐ Ⓑ Ⓒ Ⓓ   19. Ⓐ Ⓑ Ⓒ Ⓓ
4. Ⓐ Ⓑ Ⓒ Ⓓ   8. Ⓐ Ⓑ Ⓒ Ⓓ   12. Ⓐ Ⓑ Ⓒ Ⓓ   16. Ⓐ Ⓑ Ⓒ Ⓓ   20. Ⓐ Ⓑ Ⓒ Ⓓ

Pretest, part 2

1. Ⓐ Ⓑ Ⓒ Ⓓ   5. Ⓐ Ⓑ Ⓒ Ⓓ   9. Ⓐ Ⓑ Ⓒ Ⓓ   13. Ⓐ Ⓑ Ⓒ Ⓓ   17. Ⓐ Ⓑ Ⓒ Ⓓ
2. Ⓐ Ⓑ Ⓒ Ⓓ   6. Ⓐ Ⓑ Ⓒ Ⓓ   10. Ⓐ Ⓑ Ⓒ Ⓓ   14. Ⓐ Ⓑ Ⓒ Ⓓ   18. Ⓐ Ⓑ Ⓒ Ⓓ
3. Ⓐ Ⓑ Ⓒ Ⓓ   7. Ⓐ Ⓑ Ⓒ Ⓓ   11. Ⓐ Ⓑ Ⓒ Ⓓ   15. Ⓐ Ⓑ Ⓒ Ⓓ
4. Ⓐ Ⓑ Ⓒ Ⓓ   8. Ⓐ Ⓑ Ⓒ Ⓓ   12. Ⓐ Ⓑ Ⓒ Ⓓ   16. Ⓐ Ⓑ Ⓒ Ⓓ

Posttest, part 1

1. Ⓐ Ⓑ Ⓒ Ⓓ   5. Ⓐ Ⓑ Ⓒ Ⓓ   9. Ⓐ Ⓑ Ⓒ Ⓓ   13. Ⓐ Ⓑ Ⓒ Ⓓ   17. Ⓐ Ⓑ Ⓒ Ⓓ
2. Ⓐ Ⓑ Ⓒ Ⓓ   6. Ⓐ Ⓑ Ⓒ Ⓓ   10. Ⓐ Ⓑ Ⓒ Ⓓ   14. Ⓐ Ⓑ Ⓒ Ⓓ   18. Ⓐ Ⓑ Ⓒ Ⓓ
3. Ⓐ Ⓑ Ⓒ Ⓓ   7. Ⓐ Ⓑ Ⓒ Ⓓ   11. Ⓐ Ⓑ Ⓒ Ⓓ   15. Ⓐ Ⓑ Ⓒ Ⓓ   19. Ⓐ Ⓑ Ⓒ Ⓓ
4. Ⓐ Ⓑ Ⓒ Ⓓ   8. Ⓐ Ⓑ Ⓒ Ⓓ   12. Ⓐ Ⓑ Ⓒ Ⓓ   16. Ⓐ Ⓑ Ⓒ Ⓓ   20. Ⓐ Ⓑ Ⓒ Ⓓ

Posttest, part 2

1. Ⓐ Ⓑ Ⓒ Ⓓ   5. Ⓐ Ⓑ Ⓒ Ⓓ   9. Ⓐ Ⓑ Ⓒ Ⓓ   13. Ⓐ Ⓑ Ⓒ Ⓓ   17. Ⓐ Ⓑ Ⓒ Ⓓ
2. Ⓐ Ⓑ Ⓒ Ⓓ   6. Ⓐ Ⓑ Ⓒ Ⓓ   10. Ⓐ Ⓑ Ⓒ Ⓓ   14. Ⓐ Ⓑ Ⓒ Ⓓ   18. Ⓐ Ⓑ Ⓒ Ⓓ
3. Ⓐ Ⓑ Ⓒ Ⓓ   7. Ⓐ Ⓑ Ⓒ Ⓓ   11. Ⓐ Ⓑ Ⓒ Ⓓ   15. Ⓐ Ⓑ Ⓒ Ⓓ
4. Ⓐ Ⓑ Ⓒ Ⓓ   8. Ⓐ Ⓑ Ⓒ Ⓓ   12. Ⓐ Ⓑ Ⓒ Ⓓ   16. Ⓐ Ⓑ Ⓒ Ⓓ

1

Lesson 1: Number Concepts

1. Ⓐ Ⓑ Ⓒ Ⓓ	7. Ⓐ Ⓑ Ⓒ Ⓓ	13. Ⓐ Ⓑ Ⓒ Ⓓ	19. Ⓐ Ⓑ Ⓒ Ⓓ	25. Ⓐ Ⓑ Ⓒ Ⓓ
2. Ⓐ Ⓑ Ⓒ Ⓓ	8. Ⓐ Ⓑ Ⓒ Ⓓ	14. Ⓐ Ⓑ Ⓒ Ⓓ	20. Ⓐ Ⓑ Ⓒ Ⓓ	26. Ⓐ Ⓑ Ⓒ Ⓓ
3. Ⓐ Ⓑ Ⓒ Ⓓ	9. Ⓐ Ⓑ Ⓒ Ⓓ	15. Ⓐ Ⓑ Ⓒ Ⓓ	21. Ⓐ Ⓑ Ⓒ Ⓓ	27. Ⓐ Ⓑ Ⓒ Ⓓ
4. Ⓐ Ⓑ Ⓒ Ⓓ	10. Ⓐ Ⓑ Ⓒ Ⓓ	16. Ⓐ Ⓑ Ⓒ Ⓓ	22. Ⓐ Ⓑ Ⓒ Ⓓ	28. Ⓐ Ⓑ Ⓒ Ⓓ
5. Ⓐ Ⓑ Ⓒ Ⓓ	11. Ⓐ Ⓑ Ⓒ Ⓓ	17. Ⓐ Ⓑ Ⓒ Ⓓ	23. Ⓐ Ⓑ Ⓒ Ⓓ	
6. Ⓐ Ⓑ Ⓒ Ⓓ	12. Ⓐ Ⓑ Ⓒ Ⓓ	18. Ⓐ Ⓑ Ⓒ Ⓓ	24. Ⓐ Ⓑ Ⓒ Ⓓ	

Lesson 2: Whole Number Computation

1. Ⓐ Ⓑ Ⓒ Ⓓ	8. Ⓐ Ⓑ Ⓒ Ⓓ	15. Ⓐ Ⓑ Ⓒ Ⓓ	22. Ⓐ Ⓑ Ⓒ Ⓓ	29. Ⓐ Ⓑ Ⓒ Ⓓ
2. Ⓐ Ⓑ Ⓒ Ⓓ	9. Ⓐ Ⓑ Ⓒ Ⓓ	16. Ⓐ Ⓑ Ⓒ Ⓓ	23. Ⓐ Ⓑ Ⓒ Ⓓ	30. Ⓐ Ⓑ Ⓒ Ⓓ
3. Ⓐ Ⓑ Ⓒ Ⓓ	10. Ⓐ Ⓑ Ⓒ Ⓓ	17. Ⓐ Ⓑ Ⓒ Ⓓ	24. Ⓐ Ⓑ Ⓒ Ⓓ	31. Ⓐ Ⓑ Ⓒ Ⓓ
4. Ⓐ Ⓑ Ⓒ Ⓓ	11. Ⓐ Ⓑ Ⓒ Ⓓ	18. Ⓐ Ⓑ Ⓒ Ⓓ	25. Ⓐ Ⓑ Ⓒ Ⓓ	32. Ⓐ Ⓑ Ⓒ Ⓓ
5. Ⓐ Ⓑ Ⓒ Ⓓ	12. Ⓐ Ⓑ Ⓒ Ⓓ	19. Ⓐ Ⓑ Ⓒ Ⓓ	26. Ⓐ Ⓑ Ⓒ Ⓓ	
6. Ⓐ Ⓑ Ⓒ Ⓓ	13. Ⓐ Ⓑ Ⓒ Ⓓ	20. Ⓐ Ⓑ Ⓒ Ⓓ	27. Ⓐ Ⓑ Ⓒ Ⓓ	
7. Ⓐ Ⓑ Ⓒ Ⓓ	14. Ⓐ Ⓑ Ⓒ Ⓓ	21. Ⓐ Ⓑ Ⓒ Ⓓ	28. Ⓐ Ⓑ Ⓒ Ⓓ	

Lesson 3: Estimation

1. Ⓐ Ⓑ Ⓒ Ⓓ	3. Ⓐ Ⓑ Ⓒ Ⓓ	5. Ⓐ Ⓑ Ⓒ Ⓓ	7. Ⓐ Ⓑ Ⓒ Ⓓ	9. Ⓐ Ⓑ Ⓒ Ⓓ
2. Ⓐ Ⓑ Ⓒ Ⓓ	4. Ⓐ Ⓑ Ⓒ Ⓓ	6. Ⓐ Ⓑ Ⓒ Ⓓ	8. Ⓐ Ⓑ Ⓒ Ⓓ	10. Ⓐ Ⓑ Ⓒ Ⓓ

Lesson 4: Decimals and Fractions

1. Ⓐ Ⓑ Ⓒ Ⓓ	7. Ⓐ Ⓑ Ⓒ Ⓓ	13. Ⓐ Ⓑ Ⓒ Ⓓ	19. Ⓐ Ⓑ Ⓒ Ⓓ	25. Ⓐ Ⓑ Ⓒ Ⓓ
2. Ⓐ Ⓑ Ⓒ Ⓓ	8. Ⓐ Ⓑ Ⓒ Ⓓ	14. Ⓐ Ⓑ Ⓒ Ⓓ	20. Ⓐ Ⓑ Ⓒ Ⓓ	26. Ⓐ Ⓑ Ⓒ Ⓓ
3. Ⓐ Ⓑ Ⓒ Ⓓ	9. Ⓐ Ⓑ Ⓒ Ⓓ	15. Ⓐ Ⓑ Ⓒ Ⓓ	21. Ⓐ Ⓑ Ⓒ Ⓓ	27. Ⓐ Ⓑ Ⓒ Ⓓ
4. Ⓐ Ⓑ Ⓒ Ⓓ	10. Ⓐ Ⓑ Ⓒ Ⓓ	16. Ⓐ Ⓑ Ⓒ Ⓓ	22. Ⓐ Ⓑ Ⓒ Ⓓ	
5. Ⓐ Ⓑ Ⓒ Ⓓ	11. Ⓐ Ⓑ Ⓒ Ⓓ	17. Ⓐ Ⓑ Ⓒ Ⓓ	23. Ⓐ Ⓑ Ⓒ Ⓓ	
6. Ⓐ Ⓑ Ⓒ Ⓓ	12. Ⓐ Ⓑ Ⓒ Ⓓ	18. Ⓐ Ⓑ Ⓒ Ⓓ	24. Ⓐ Ⓑ Ⓒ Ⓓ	

Lesson 5: Measurement

1. Ⓐ Ⓑ Ⓒ Ⓓ	4. Ⓐ Ⓑ Ⓒ Ⓓ	7. Ⓐ Ⓑ Ⓒ Ⓓ	10. Ⓐ Ⓑ Ⓒ Ⓓ
2. Ⓐ Ⓑ Ⓒ Ⓓ	5. Ⓐ Ⓑ Ⓒ Ⓓ	8. Ⓐ Ⓑ Ⓒ Ⓓ	11. Ⓐ Ⓑ Ⓒ Ⓓ
3. Ⓐ Ⓑ Ⓒ Ⓓ	6. Ⓐ Ⓑ Ⓒ Ⓓ	9. Ⓐ Ⓑ Ⓒ Ⓓ	12. Ⓐ Ⓑ Ⓒ Ⓓ

Lesson 6: Geometry

1. Ⓐ Ⓑ Ⓒ Ⓓ	6. Ⓐ Ⓑ Ⓒ Ⓓ	11. Ⓐ Ⓑ Ⓒ Ⓓ	16. Ⓐ Ⓑ Ⓒ Ⓓ	21. Ⓐ Ⓑ Ⓒ Ⓓ
2. Ⓐ Ⓑ Ⓒ Ⓓ	7. Ⓐ Ⓑ Ⓒ Ⓓ	12. Ⓐ Ⓑ Ⓒ Ⓓ	17. Ⓐ Ⓑ Ⓒ Ⓓ	22. Ⓐ Ⓑ Ⓒ Ⓓ
3. Ⓐ Ⓑ Ⓒ Ⓓ	8. Ⓐ Ⓑ Ⓒ Ⓓ	13. Ⓐ Ⓑ Ⓒ Ⓓ	18. Ⓐ Ⓑ Ⓒ Ⓓ	23. Ⓐ Ⓑ Ⓒ Ⓓ
4. Ⓐ Ⓑ Ⓒ Ⓓ	9. Ⓐ Ⓑ Ⓒ Ⓓ	14. Ⓐ Ⓑ Ⓒ Ⓓ	19. Ⓐ Ⓑ Ⓒ Ⓓ	24. Ⓐ Ⓑ Ⓒ Ⓓ
5. Ⓐ Ⓑ Ⓒ Ⓓ	10. Ⓐ Ⓑ Ⓒ Ⓓ	15. Ⓐ Ⓑ Ⓒ Ⓓ	20. Ⓐ Ⓑ Ⓒ Ⓓ	

Lesson 7: Charts and Graphs

1. Ⓐ Ⓑ Ⓒ Ⓓ	4. Ⓐ Ⓑ Ⓒ Ⓓ	7. Ⓐ Ⓑ Ⓒ Ⓓ	10. Ⓐ Ⓑ Ⓒ Ⓓ	13. Ⓐ Ⓑ Ⓒ Ⓓ
2. Ⓐ Ⓑ Ⓒ Ⓓ	5. Ⓐ Ⓑ Ⓒ Ⓓ	8. Ⓐ Ⓑ Ⓒ Ⓓ	11. Ⓐ Ⓑ Ⓒ Ⓓ	14. Ⓐ Ⓑ Ⓒ Ⓓ
3. Ⓐ Ⓑ Ⓒ Ⓓ	6. Ⓐ Ⓑ Ⓒ Ⓓ	9. Ⓐ Ⓑ Ⓒ Ⓓ	12. Ⓐ Ⓑ Ⓒ Ⓓ	

Lesson 8: Probability

1. Ⓐ Ⓑ Ⓒ Ⓓ	2. Ⓐ Ⓑ Ⓒ Ⓓ

Lesson 9: Problem-Solving Strategies

1. Ⓐ Ⓑ Ⓒ Ⓓ	6. Ⓐ Ⓑ Ⓒ Ⓓ	11. Ⓐ Ⓑ Ⓒ Ⓓ	16. Ⓐ Ⓑ Ⓒ Ⓓ	21. Ⓐ Ⓑ Ⓒ Ⓓ
2. Ⓐ Ⓑ Ⓒ Ⓓ	7. Ⓐ Ⓑ Ⓒ Ⓓ	12. Ⓐ Ⓑ Ⓒ Ⓓ	17. Ⓐ Ⓑ Ⓒ Ⓓ	
3. Ⓐ Ⓑ Ⓒ Ⓓ	8. Ⓐ Ⓑ Ⓒ Ⓓ	13. Ⓐ Ⓑ Ⓒ Ⓓ	18. Ⓐ Ⓑ Ⓒ Ⓓ	
4. Ⓐ Ⓑ Ⓒ Ⓓ	9. Ⓐ Ⓑ Ⓒ Ⓓ	14. Ⓐ Ⓑ Ⓒ Ⓓ	19. Ⓐ Ⓑ Ⓒ Ⓓ	
5. Ⓐ Ⓑ Ⓒ Ⓓ	10. Ⓐ Ⓑ Ⓒ Ⓓ	15. Ⓐ Ⓑ Ⓒ Ⓓ	20. Ⓐ Ⓑ Ⓒ Ⓓ	

Lesson 10: Problem Solving

1. Ⓐ Ⓑ Ⓒ Ⓓ	6. Ⓐ Ⓑ Ⓒ Ⓓ	11. Ⓐ Ⓑ Ⓒ Ⓓ	16. Ⓐ Ⓑ Ⓒ Ⓓ	21. Ⓐ Ⓑ Ⓒ Ⓓ
2. Ⓐ Ⓑ Ⓒ Ⓓ	7. Ⓐ Ⓑ Ⓒ Ⓓ	12. Ⓐ Ⓑ Ⓒ Ⓓ	17. Ⓐ Ⓑ Ⓒ Ⓓ	22. Ⓐ Ⓑ Ⓒ Ⓓ
3. Ⓐ Ⓑ Ⓒ Ⓓ	8. Ⓐ Ⓑ Ⓒ Ⓓ	13. Ⓐ Ⓑ Ⓒ Ⓓ	18. Ⓐ Ⓑ Ⓒ Ⓓ	23. Ⓐ Ⓑ Ⓒ Ⓓ
4. Ⓐ Ⓑ Ⓒ Ⓓ	9. Ⓐ Ⓑ Ⓒ Ⓓ	14. Ⓐ Ⓑ Ⓒ Ⓓ	19. Ⓐ Ⓑ Ⓒ Ⓓ	24. Ⓐ Ⓑ Ⓒ Ⓓ
5. Ⓐ Ⓑ Ⓒ Ⓓ	10. Ⓐ Ⓑ Ⓒ Ⓓ	15. Ⓐ Ⓑ Ⓒ Ⓓ	20. Ⓐ Ⓑ Ⓒ Ⓓ	

Pretest, part 1

You have 20 minutes to complete this test.

Lesson 1: Number Concepts

Directions Darken the circle by the correct answer to each problem.

1. Which number is two thousand six hundred sixty-four?
   - Ⓐ 2,646
   - Ⓑ 2,604
   - Ⓒ 2,664
   - Ⓓ 26,604

2. Which of these groups of numbers is ordered from greatest to smallest?
   - Ⓐ 652, 745, 29
   - Ⓑ 29, 652, 745
   - Ⓒ 745, 652, 29
   - Ⓓ 745, 29, 645

3. Estimate the sum of 619 + 296.
   - Ⓐ 900
   - Ⓑ 800
   - Ⓒ 920
   - Ⓓ 890

4. What number should come next?
   36, 42, 48, 54, _____
   - Ⓐ 55
   - Ⓑ 56
   - Ⓒ 58
   - Ⓓ 60

Lesson 2: Whole Number Computation

Directions Darken the circle by the correct answer to each problem.

5.
$$
\begin{array}{r}
551 \\
+\ 344 \\
\hline
\end{array}
$$
   - Ⓐ 813
   - Ⓑ 895
   - Ⓒ 886
   - Ⓓ 210

6.
$$
\begin{array}{r}
1,079 \\
-\ 382 \\
\hline
\end{array}
$$
   - Ⓐ 697
   - Ⓑ 607
   - Ⓒ 679
   - Ⓓ 1,461

GO ON ⇨

Pretest, part 1, page 2

7. 201
    × 35

    Ⓐ 7,350
    Ⓑ 7,530
    Ⓒ 7,035
    Ⓓ 7,053

8. 12 ⟌ 528

    Ⓐ 43 R4
    Ⓑ 45
    Ⓒ 43 R1
    Ⓓ 44

Lesson 3: Estimation

Directions Darken the circle by the best estimate for each problem.

9. Which number shows 45,831 rounded to the nearest thousand?
    Ⓐ 46,000
    Ⓑ 45,800
    Ⓒ 45,000
    Ⓓ 45,900

10. Mrs. Schroeder's rose farm had 527 rosebushes. She sold 215 of them. Which is the best estimate of the number of rosebushes she has left?

    Ⓐ 100
    Ⓑ 200
    Ⓒ 300
    Ⓓ 400

Lesson 4: Decimals and Fractions

Directions Darken the circle by the correct answer to each problem.

11. 1.3
    − 0.8

    Ⓐ 0.5
    Ⓑ 1.5
    Ⓒ 50
    Ⓓ 2.1

12. What decimal shows the part of this figure that is shaded?
    Ⓐ 0.81
    Ⓑ 1.9
    Ⓒ 0.19
    Ⓓ 0.019

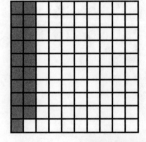

GO ON ⇨

Pretest, part 1, page 3

13.　　　$0.45
　　　+ 0.83

　　Ⓐ $1.28
　　Ⓑ $2.28
　　Ⓒ 0.78
　　Ⓓ $1.82

14. Which shaded area shows $\frac{2}{3}$?
　　Ⓐ A
　　Ⓑ B
　　Ⓒ C
　　Ⓓ D

　　A　　B　　C　　D

15. $7\frac{3}{7} + 2\frac{2}{7} =$
　　Ⓐ $10\frac{2}{7}$
　　Ⓑ $9\frac{5}{7}$
　　Ⓒ $5\frac{2}{7}$
　　Ⓓ $5\frac{1}{7}$

16. $9\frac{4}{6} - 5\frac{1}{6} =$
　　Ⓐ $4\frac{1}{2}$
　　Ⓑ $5\frac{1}{2}$
　　Ⓒ $4\frac{5}{6}$
　　Ⓓ $14\frac{5}{6}$

Lesson 5: Measurement

Directions Darken the circle by the correct answer to each problem.

17. Which unit of measurement would be best to determine the length of a soccer field?
　　Ⓐ meters
　　Ⓑ liters
　　Ⓒ grams
　　Ⓓ kilometers

18. Which of these has a weight that is best measured in grams?
　　Ⓐ a cookie
　　Ⓑ a bag of potatoes
　　Ⓒ a refrigerator
　　Ⓓ a car

19. How many inches are there between point B and point A?
　　Ⓐ $1\frac{1}{2}$ inches
　　Ⓑ 3 inches
　　Ⓒ 1 inch
　　Ⓓ $2\frac{1}{2}$ inches

20. The first clock shows the time Cody left school. The second clock shows the time she arrived home. How many minutes did it take her to walk home?
　　Ⓐ 5
　　Ⓑ 20
　　Ⓒ 30
　　Ⓓ 35

STOP

Your score: _____

Pretest, part 2

You have 25 minutes to complete this test.

Lesson 6: Geometry

Directions Darken the circle by the correct answer to each question.

1. What is the name of this figure?
   - Ⓐ pentagon
   - Ⓑ triangle
   - Ⓒ parallelogram
   - Ⓓ square

2. Which of these lines are intersecting?

3. What is the perimeter of this figure?
   - Ⓐ 223 yards
   - Ⓑ 263 yards
   - Ⓒ 300 yards
   - Ⓓ 258 yards

   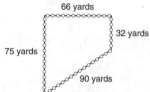

4. What is the area of the shaded area in square units?
   - Ⓐ 20 sq. units
   - Ⓑ 35 sq. units
   - Ⓒ 45 sq. units
   - Ⓓ 30 sq. units

Lesson 7: Charts and Graphs

Directions Darken the circle by the correct answer to each question.

Use this graph to answer questions 5 and 6.

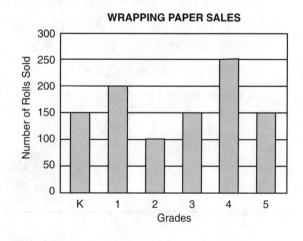

5. How many rolls of wrapping paper did the students in grade 3 sell?
   - Ⓐ 100 rolls
   - Ⓑ 150 rolls
   - Ⓒ 200 rolls
   - Ⓓ 250 rolls

6. How many rolls were sold by grades 2, 3, and 4 altogether?
   - Ⓐ 400 rolls
   - Ⓑ 650 rolls
   - Ⓒ 300 rolls
   - Ⓓ 500 rolls

GO ON ⇨

6

Pretest, part 2, page 2

Lesson 8: Probability

Directions Darken the circle by the correct answer to each question.

7. If the spinner shown here is spun 8 times, which number will it probably point to most often?

Ⓐ 4
Ⓑ 3
Ⓒ 2
Ⓓ 1

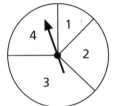

8. Michael can separate his compact discs into 4 equal groups with none left over. How many compact discs could Michael have?

Ⓐ 12
Ⓑ 15
Ⓒ 21
Ⓓ 27

Lesson 9: Problem-Solving Strategies

Directions Choose the best strategy to solve each problem.

9. There are 528 seats in the new multiplex movie theater. All of the seats are usually filled 4 days each week. About how many people fill the theater each week?

Ⓐ estimate
Ⓑ make a graph
Ⓒ work backwards
Ⓓ more than one step

10. Gino's mother makes 24 cupcakes for a party. Gino and 5 friends eat 3 cupcakes each. How many cupcakes are left?

Ⓐ extra information
Ⓑ more than one step
Ⓒ make a list
Ⓓ look for a pattern

11. Derek bought 6 report folders. Each folder cost $0.39. He gave the clerk $3.00. How much change did he receive?

Ⓐ make a list
Ⓑ extra information
Ⓒ more than one step
Ⓓ estimate

12. Roberto has an orange cat and a white cat. He has black, brown, and white collars for his cats. How many different ways can he use the collars for his cats?

Ⓐ make a drawing
Ⓑ estimation
Ⓒ more than one step
Ⓓ make a list

GO ON ⇨

Pretest, part 2, page 3

Lesson 10: Problem Solving

Directions Darken the circle by the correct answer to each problem.

13. Donna enjoys doing watercolor painting. At the craft store, she had to decide between buying a paint set for $4 or a set for $7. How many more paints are in the $7 set?

Ⓐ 18
Ⓑ 10
Ⓒ 28
Ⓓ 8

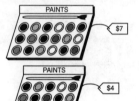

14. Kelsey is redecorating her room. She bought two throw pillows for $12.47 each and a framed poster for $35.95. How much did she spend in all?

Ⓐ $61.89
Ⓑ $48.42
Ⓒ $60.89
Ⓓ $50.42

15. Meg's sticker album has 36 pages. She would like to put 12 stickers on each page. How many stickers will she need to fill the album?

Ⓐ 38
Ⓑ 432
Ⓒ 378
Ⓓ 492

16. Maleek bought a glue stick for 39¢ and a protractor for 59¢. If he does not have to pay tax, how much change should he get back from $1.00?

Ⓐ 2¢
Ⓑ 12¢
Ⓒ 88¢
Ⓓ 98¢

17. The cost of some computer software is between $60 and $70. The sum of the digits is 18. Which could be the price of the software?

Ⓐ $57.80
Ⓑ $60.78
Ⓒ $66.60
Ⓓ $76.50

18. Which number is divisible by both 5 and 2?

Ⓐ 365
Ⓑ 240
Ⓒ 334
Ⓓ 781

Your score: _____

Posttest, part 1

You have 20 minutes to complete this test.

Lesson 1: Number Concepts

Directions Darken the circle by the correct answer to each problem.

1. Which of these is another way to write 20,483?
   - Ⓐ 20,000 + 400 + 80 + 3
   - Ⓑ 20,000 + 438 + 3
   - Ⓒ 20,000 + 48 + 83
   - Ⓓ 20,000 + 84 + 3

2. Which of these number sentences is true?
   - Ⓐ 4,156 > 4,257
   - Ⓑ 8,651 = 8,000 + 600 + 15
   - Ⓒ 375 < 379
   - Ⓓ 1,332 > 1,432

3. What does the 4 in 9,742 mean?
   - Ⓐ four hundred
   - Ⓑ four
   - Ⓒ forty
   - Ⓓ four thousand

4. Look at the pattern shown here. Which number is missing?
   101, 105, _____ , 113, 117
   - Ⓐ 107
   - Ⓑ 110
   - Ⓒ 112
   - Ⓓ 109

Lesson 2: Whole Number Computation

Directions Darken the circle by the correct answer to each problem.

5.
```
    575
    428
+   358
_____
```
   - Ⓐ 1,361
   - Ⓑ 1,272
   - Ⓒ 1,341
   - Ⓓ 1,316

6.
```
  1,985
-    98
_____
```
   - Ⓐ 1,787
   - Ⓑ 1,897
   - Ⓒ 1,887
   - Ⓓ 2,083

GO ON ⇨

Posttest, part 1, page 2

7. 89
       × 9

   Ⓐ 801
   Ⓑ 810
   Ⓒ 811
   Ⓓ 899

8. 7)1,904

   Ⓐ 270 R2
   Ⓑ 227
   Ⓒ 272
   Ⓓ 197

Lesson 3: Estimation

Directions Darken the circle by the best estimate for each problem.

9. There are 1910 pages in a 3-volume history of Texas. What is the number rounded to the nearest hundred?
   Ⓐ 1000
   Ⓑ 1900
   Ⓒ 900
   Ⓓ 1300

10. Eliot enjoys exercise. It usually takes him 9 minutes to jog a mile. Which is the closest estimate of how long it would take Eliot to jog 5 miles?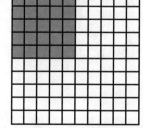
   Ⓐ between 20 and 30 minutes
   Ⓑ between 30 and 40 minutes
   Ⓒ between 40 and 50 minutes
   Ⓓ between 50 and 60 minutes

Lesson 4: Decimals and Fractions

Directions Darken the circle by the correct answer to each problem.

11. 2.60
       − 0.95

   Ⓐ 6.50
   Ⓑ 1.605
   Ⓒ 1.65
   Ⓓ 3.55

12. Which decimal shows the part of this figure that is shaded?
   Ⓐ 0.75
   Ⓑ 1.25
   Ⓒ 0.25
   Ⓓ 0.45

GO ON ⇨

Posttest
Higher Scores on Math Standardized Tests 4, SV 2063-X

Posttest, part 1, page 3

13. $1.25
      $\times$ 30

Ⓐ $37.50

Ⓑ $375.00

Ⓒ $37.05

Ⓓ $31.25

14. $\frac{1}{2} + \frac{3}{8} =$

Ⓐ $\frac{4}{8}$

Ⓑ $\frac{7}{8}$

Ⓒ $\frac{4}{10}$

Ⓓ $\frac{4}{16}$

15. Which shaded part shows the greatest fraction?

Ⓐ $= \frac{4}{6}$ Ⓑ ▭ $= \frac{1}{3}$

Ⓒ ▦ $= \frac{8}{9}$ Ⓓ ▭ $= \frac{1}{2}$

16. $\frac{5}{6} \times \frac{3}{4} =$

Ⓐ $\frac{8}{10}$

Ⓑ $\frac{2}{20}$

Ⓒ $\frac{5}{8}$

Ⓓ $\frac{1}{6}$

Lesson 5: Measurement

Directions Darken the circle by the correct answer to each problem.

17. The bus will leave at 2:20. The picture shows what time it is now. How many minutes until the bus leaves?

Ⓐ 20

Ⓑ 25

Ⓒ 30

Ⓓ 35

18. What unit of measurement would be best to use to measure the width of a window?

Ⓐ inches

Ⓑ yards

Ⓒ rods

Ⓓ miles

19. What would be the best unit to use to measure the amount of juice in a pitcher?

Ⓐ meter

Ⓑ liter

Ⓒ kilometer

Ⓓ gram

20. How many centimeters are there between point J and point K?

Ⓐ $1\frac{1}{2}$

Ⓑ 3

Ⓒ $3\frac{1}{2}$

Ⓓ 5

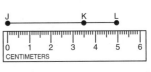

Your score: _____

Posttest, part 2

You have 25 minutes to complete this test.

Lesson 6: Geometry

Directions Darken the circle by the correct answer to each question.

1. What is the perimeter of this chalkboard if it is expressed in feet?

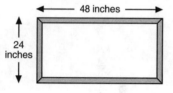

   Ⓐ 12 feet
   Ⓑ 8 feet
   Ⓒ 20 feet
   Ⓓ 10 feet

2. What is the area of the shaded figure in square units?

   Ⓐ 25
   Ⓑ 30
   Ⓒ 35
   Ⓓ 40

3. Which pair of lines appear to be parallel?

   Ⓐ AB and CD
   Ⓑ AC and BD
   Ⓒ AC and AB
   Ⓓ CD and BD

4. Which best represents a pair of congruent shapes?

   Ⓐ   Ⓑ Z N

   Ⓒ   Ⓓ H I

Lesson 7: Charts and Graphs

Directions Darken the circle by the correct answer to each question.

This graph shows the average temperature in River Town. **Use the graph to answer questions 5 and 6.**

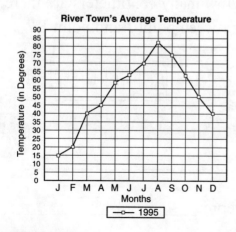

5. What was the average temperature in December?

   Ⓐ 40°
   Ⓑ 45°
   Ⓒ 50°
   Ⓓ 35°

6. In which month was the average temperature 70°?

   Ⓐ June
   Ⓑ July
   Ⓒ August
   Ⓓ September

GO ON ⇨

Posttest, part 2, page 2

Lesson 8: Probability

Directions Darken the circle by the correct answer to each problem.

7. Wen is playing a game with the spinner shown here. If it is spun 6 times, which animal will it probably point to most often?
   Ⓐ Dolphin
   Ⓑ Panther
   Ⓒ Otter
   Ⓓ Monkey

8. Reilly can put his crayons into 4 equal groups without any left over. Choose the number of crayons he could have.
   Ⓐ 20
   Ⓑ 14
   Ⓒ 18
   Ⓓ 15

Lesson 9: Problem-Solving Strategies

Directions Choose the best strategy to solve each problem.

9. Ms. Casey gave the class 120 math exercises to do. Lenore finished 56 of them at school. How many did she have left to do at home?
   Ⓐ make a list
   Ⓑ guess and check
   Ⓒ use a pattern
   Ⓓ work backwards

10. Sheo is older than Jay. Sally is younger than Jay. Maria's age is between Sally's and Sheo's. Who is the youngest?
    Ⓐ estimation
    Ⓑ make a list
    Ⓒ look for a pattern
    Ⓓ extra information

11. There are 26 students in Mr. Samuels' fourth grade class. He ordered 21 calendars for each student to sell for a fund raiser. How many calendars did he order in all?
    Ⓐ write a number sentence
    Ⓑ make a graph
    Ⓒ make a table
    Ⓓ make a list

12. Ms. Wang makes a chocolate cake for her family of 6. She cuts the cake into 12 slices. How many slices can each person have?
    Ⓐ make a drawing
    Ⓑ estimation
    Ⓒ two-step
    Ⓓ extra information

GO ON ⇨

Posttest, part 2, page 3

Lesson 10: Problem Solving

Directions Darken the circle by the correct answer to each problem.

13. Ryan scored 129 points in his first game at the bowling alley and 132 points in his second game. How many points did Ryan score altogether?

Ⓐ 251
Ⓑ 261
Ⓒ 369
Ⓓ 161

14. LuAnne works at the hospital for 6 hours a day, every day of the week. How many hours does she work each week?

Ⓐ 30
Ⓑ 36
Ⓒ 42
Ⓓ 67

15. Earl took a bike trip. He rode 46 miles one day, and 49 miles the next day. How many miles did he ride altogether?

Ⓐ 83
Ⓑ 95
Ⓒ 109
Ⓓ 85

16. Dana's family has 8 pens to hold the 128 sheep they raise. If they put the same number of sheep in each pen, how many sheep will be in each pen?

Ⓐ 16
Ⓑ 18
Ⓒ 20
Ⓓ 13

17. Fiona wants to buy a stereo that is priced at $99.95. She has saved $55.49. How much more money does Fiona need to buy the stereo?

Ⓐ $44.46
Ⓑ $45.59
Ⓒ $54.45
Ⓓ $34.46

18. Ling read 110 pages of a novel on Friday and 216 pages on Saturday. If it takes her about 3 minutes to read a page of that book, how many minutes did she spend reading on Friday and Saturday altogether?

Ⓐ 326
Ⓑ 330
Ⓒ 672
Ⓓ 978

Your score: _____

Lesson 1: Number Concepts

Directions Darken the circle by the correct answer
to each problem.

⭐ **Testing Tips**

1. Read each question carefully to make sure you understand exactly what to do.
2. Study all the choices before you decide on the correct answer.
3. If a pattern is used, think about what would come next in the pattern.

Sample:

Which of these numbers is greater
than the others?

Ⓐ 867

Ⓑ 853

Ⓒ 876

Ⓓ 870

Answer

The correct answer is *C. 876.* 876 is
greater than any of the other numbers.

🕐 **Now Try These** *You have 25 minutes.*

1. Which of these groups of numbers
   is ordered from least to greatest?
   Ⓐ 116, 97, 89
   Ⓑ 8, 9, 116
   Ⓒ 97, 89, 116
   Ⓓ 89, 116, 97

2. There are 100 books in all on four
   shelves of a bookcase. If the same
   number of books is on each shelf,
   how many books are on the
   third shelf?
   Ⓐ 100
   Ⓑ 25
   Ⓒ 50
   Ⓓ 75

3. What is another way to write the
   numeral in the box?

   | One thousand seventeen |

   Ⓐ 117
   Ⓑ 1,107
   Ⓒ 1,117
   Ⓓ 1,017

4. Which of these is another way
   to write 1,234?
   Ⓐ 10 + 20 + 34
   Ⓑ 100 + 200 + 30 +4
   Ⓒ 1,000 + 200 + 30 + 4
   Ⓓ 1,200 + 30 + 4

GO ON ⇨

Lesson 1, page 2

5. Which of these has a 2 in the ten thousands place?
- Ⓐ 2,491
- Ⓑ 1,792,537
- Ⓒ 26,702
- Ⓓ 31,284

6. Which of these is ten thousand fifty-eight?
- Ⓐ 10,508
- Ⓑ 1,058
- Ⓒ 10,805
- Ⓓ 10,058

7. Which number sentence shows the correct placement of the < or > sign?
- Ⓐ 415 > 515
- Ⓑ 749 < 721
- Ⓒ 5 < 1
- Ⓓ 45 > 41

8. What is another way to write the numeral in the box?

| 56 |

- Ⓐ five-six
- Ⓑ five-sixty
- Ⓒ sixty-five
- Ⓓ fifty-six

9. What time is four hours after 3:15 P.M.?
- Ⓐ 7:00 P.M.
- Ⓑ 1:17 P.M.
- Ⓒ 7:15 P.M.
- Ⓓ 6:45 P.M.

10. What number completes this pattern?
28, 35, 42, 49, _____
- Ⓐ 53
- Ⓑ 61
- Ⓒ 59
- Ⓓ 56

11. Which of the following groups of numbers has all even numbers?
- Ⓐ 36, 71, 56
- Ⓑ 62, 10, 78
- Ⓒ 36, 43, 10
- Ⓓ 45, 61, 83

12. Which numeral fits best in the box?
793 < ☐
- Ⓐ 740
- Ⓑ 791
- Ⓒ 796
- Ⓓ 787

13. Heather separated her ducklings into 5 equal groups, with none left out. How many ducklings *could* she have?
- Ⓐ 27
- Ⓑ 19
- Ⓒ 16
- Ⓓ 20

GO ON ⇨

Name _____ Date _____

Lesson 1, page 3

14. What number makes this number sentence true?

$(4 + 6) + 2 = (6 + \Box) + 2$

Ⓐ 0
Ⓑ 2
Ⓒ 4
Ⓓ 6

15. Which figure is missing in this pattern? ☆ ☆ ○ ○ △ _ □ □

Ⓐ star
Ⓑ square
Ⓒ circle
Ⓓ triangle

16. If you continue this pattern, how many more dots would the next group have?

Ⓐ 5 more dots
Ⓑ 4 more dots
Ⓒ 3 more dots
Ⓓ 6 more dots

17. What is the missing number in this pattern?

50, 45, 40, _____, 30, 25

Ⓐ 41
Ⓑ 39
Ⓒ 35
Ⓓ 31

18. Which numeral makes this sentence true?

$249 < \Box$

Ⓐ 214
Ⓑ 237
Ⓒ 241
Ⓓ 256

19. Which of the following numbers is even?

Ⓐ 336
Ⓑ 873
Ⓒ 729
Ⓓ 645

20. Which of these is the same as DCXXVI?

Ⓐ 525
Ⓑ 621
Ⓒ 1,521
Ⓓ 626

21. Which number sentence belongs to the same fact family as $8 \times 4 = \Box$?

Ⓐ $8 \div \Box = 4$
Ⓑ $8 \div 4 = \Box$
Ⓒ $\Box \div 4 = 8$
Ⓓ $4 \div \Box = 8$

GO ON ⇨

Lesson 1, page 4

22. What number should go in the ☐ to make the number sentence true?

$(3 + 5) + 7 = 3 + (\square + 7)$

Ⓐ 3
Ⓑ 5
Ⓒ 7
Ⓓ 8

23. What number makes both number sentences true?

$8 \times ? = 48$

$23 + ? = 29$

Ⓐ 6
Ⓑ 8
Ⓒ 7
Ⓓ 9

24. Which of the following numbers is odd?

Ⓐ 138
Ⓑ 413
Ⓒ 756
Ⓓ 294

25. Which number goes in the box on the number line?

Ⓐ 180
Ⓑ 200
Ⓒ 210
Ⓓ 190

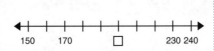

150   170   ☐   230 240

26. Apple pies at the harvest festival were cut into 5 equal portions. There were 45 portions in all. Which number sentence should you use to find out how many pies were served?

Ⓐ $45 + 5 = ?$
Ⓑ $45 \div 5 = ?$
Ⓒ $45 \times 5 = ?$
Ⓓ $45 - 5 = ?$

27. What number makes both number sentences true?

$0 \div 5 = ?$

$? \times 7 = 0$

Ⓐ 0
Ⓑ 5
Ⓒ 7
Ⓓ 35

28. Which number is less than 968 and greater than 961?

Ⓐ 970
Ⓑ 960
Ⓒ 969
Ⓓ 964

Your time: _____   Number right:_____

On this lesson I did _____ because _____

_____ .

Name _____ Date _____

Lesson 2: Whole Number Computation

Directions Darken the circle by the correct answer to each problem.

 **Testing Tips**

1. Check the sign to make sure you are doing the correct operation.
2. Estimate the answer.
3. Cross out any choices that must be wrong.
4. Check your work.

Sample:

$307 + 28 + 459 =$

Ⓐ 894

Ⓑ 1,046

Ⓒ 794

Ⓓ 774

Answer

The correct answer is *C. 794*. You can estimate the sum at about 830. Now you know that the other answers would not be correct.

Now Try These   *You have 30 minutes.*

1.   78,321
     +   89
     _____

Ⓐ 79,400

Ⓑ 78,400

Ⓒ 78,410

Ⓓ 79,369

2.   495
       830
     + 185
     _____

Ⓐ 1,610

Ⓑ 1,500

Ⓒ 1,510

Ⓓ 1,600

3. $45 + 29 + 732 =$

Ⓐ 716

Ⓑ 806

Ⓒ 816

Ⓓ 706

4.   29,630
     −   5,834
     _____

Ⓐ 23,794

Ⓑ 23,704

Ⓒ 24,796

Ⓓ 23,796

GO ON ⇨

Lesson 2, page 2

5.   55,261
+ 60,442

Ⓐ 115,103
Ⓑ 114,703
Ⓒ 115,703
Ⓓ 114,603

6. 1,043 + 6,807 =
Ⓐ 7,859
Ⓑ 7,850
Ⓒ 7,749
Ⓓ 5,764

7.   34,898
− 1,289

Ⓐ 33,609
Ⓑ 34,610
Ⓒ 33,619
Ⓓ 36,187

8.   10,360
−   2

Ⓐ 10,362
Ⓑ 10,358
Ⓒ 10,368
Ⓓ 20,720

9. 152 − 143 =
Ⓐ 295
Ⓑ 19
Ⓒ 298
Ⓓ 9

10.   962
− 538

Ⓐ 436
Ⓑ 444
Ⓒ 424
Ⓓ 1,500

11. 53 × 70 =
Ⓐ 3,710
Ⓑ 37,210
Ⓒ 7,210
Ⓓ 5,370

12. 60 ÷ 2 =
Ⓐ 120
Ⓑ 180
Ⓒ 30
Ⓓ 12

13. 79 × 24 =
Ⓐ 1,896
Ⓑ 1,836
Ⓒ 134
Ⓓ 2,479

14. 7)‾77‾
Ⓐ 10
Ⓑ 7
Ⓒ 11
Ⓓ 17

GO ON ⇨

Lesson 2: Whole Number Computation
Higher Scores on Math Standardized Tests 4, SV 2063-X

Lesson 2, page 3

15. $6{,}409 \div 7 =$
- Ⓐ 915 R4
- Ⓑ 915
- Ⓒ 885 R7
- Ⓓ 9,154

16.
$$\begin{array}{r} 324 \\ 820 \\ +\ \ 408 \\ \hline \end{array}$$
- Ⓐ 1,542
- Ⓑ 1,642
- Ⓒ 1,552
- Ⓓ 1,652

17. $82 + 38 =$
- Ⓐ 122
- Ⓑ 110
- Ⓒ 120
- Ⓓ 44

18. $12\overline{)528}$
- Ⓐ 44
- Ⓑ 54
- Ⓒ 43 R4
- Ⓓ 96

19.
$$\begin{array}{r} 540 \\ \times\ \ 9 \\ \hline \end{array}$$
- Ⓐ 5,060
- Ⓑ 4,536
- Ⓒ 4,860
- Ⓓ 5,409

20. $15\overline{)3{,}115}$
- Ⓐ 208
- Ⓑ 207 R10
- Ⓒ 209
- Ⓓ 315

21. $568 \div 9 =$
- Ⓐ 64
- Ⓑ 63 R3
- Ⓒ 63 R2
- Ⓓ 63 R1

22. $69 \times 41 =$
- Ⓐ 2,829
- Ⓑ 2,927
- Ⓒ 2,728
- Ⓓ 110

23.
$$\begin{array}{r} 11 \\ \times\ \ 97 \\ \hline \end{array}$$
- Ⓐ 1,000
- Ⓑ 1,067
- Ⓒ 1,097
- Ⓓ 197

24. $45 + 29 + 732 =$
- Ⓐ 806
- Ⓑ 716
- Ⓒ 816
- Ⓓ 608

GO ON ⇨

Lesson 2, page 4

25. $83 \times 9 =$
- Ⓐ 647
- Ⓑ 847
- Ⓒ 747
- Ⓓ 839

26. $7 \times 2 \times 2 =$
- Ⓐ 28
- Ⓑ 16
- Ⓒ 11
- Ⓓ 722

27. $46 \times 30 =$
- Ⓐ 1,308
- Ⓑ 1,038
- Ⓒ 1,380
- Ⓓ 1,830

28. $26 \div 2 =$
- Ⓐ 13
- Ⓑ 12
- Ⓒ 9
- Ⓓ 52

29. $57 \div 3 =$
- Ⓐ 18 R2
- Ⓑ 19
- Ⓒ 9
- Ⓓ 15

30. $46 \overline{)9,866}$
- Ⓐ 206
- Ⓑ 184
- Ⓒ 214 R22
- Ⓓ 214 R12

31. Donna's new photo album has 72 pages. If she puts 9 pictures on each page, how many pictures can she put in the entire album?
- Ⓐ 650 pictures
- Ⓑ 81 pictures
- Ⓒ 648 pictures
- Ⓓ 638 pictures

32. Tammy picked 120 boxes of strawberries last week and earned $85. This week she picked 150 boxes and earned $115. How much did she earn for the two weeks?
- Ⓐ $265
- Ⓑ $205
- Ⓒ $235
- Ⓓ $200

Your time: _____ Number right: _____

On this lesson I did _____ because _____

_____.

Lesson 3: Estimation

Directions Darken the circle by the answer that is the best estimate or nearest round rumber.

Testing Tips

1. Round up to the nearest ten if a number ends in 5 or more.
2. Round up if the tens are 50 or more. Do the same if the hundreds are 500 or more.
3. Round numbers when you estimate.
4. Remember that the word *about* means an exact answer is not needed.

Sample:

Round 428 to the nearest hundred.

- (A) 400
- (B) 500
- (C) 300
- (D) 450

Answer

The correct answer is *A. 400.* 428 is closer to 400 than to 500, so you do not round up.

Now Try These *You have 10 minutes.*

1. Round 526 to the nearest ten.
   - (A) 500
   - (B) 530
   - (C) 520
   - (D) 600

2. Estimate the difference between 81 and 49.
   - (A) 30
   - (B) 40
   - (C) 50
   - (D) 60

3. Estimate the product of 38 × 4.
   - (A) 120
   - (B) 110
   - (C) 160
   - (D) 180

4. Which numbers should you use to estimate 494 + 176?
   - (A) 400 + 200
   - (B) 500 + 200
   - (C) 500 + 100
   - (D) 400 + 100

GO ON ⇨

Lesson 3, page 2

5. Estimate the sum of 19, 21, and 29.
  Ⓐ 50
  Ⓑ 40
  Ⓒ 60
  Ⓓ 70

6. Diego's German shepherd puppy weighs 17.39 kilograms. What is the puppy's weight rounded to the nearest kilogram?
  Ⓐ 18 kilograms
  Ⓑ 17.4 kilograms
  Ⓒ 20 kilograms
  Ⓓ 17 kilograms

7. A group of 79 fourth-grade students and 98 third-grade students are going on a field trip. The cafeteria is supplying bag lunches for all the students. They are also supplying small packages of trail mix for a snack. About how many packages of trail mix will they need?
  Ⓐ 210 packages
  Ⓑ 80 packages
  Ⓒ 100 packages
  Ⓓ 180 packages

8. Keisha bought a package of baseball cards for $1.50, a kite for $3.99, and string for $1.75. If the cost of tax is included, *about* how much did Keisha spend altogether?
  Ⓐ $11
  Ⓑ $8
  Ⓒ $6
  Ⓓ $5

9. It takes about 4 minutes to walk around the track at the sports stadium. Which is the closest estimate of the amount of time it will take to walk around the track 7 times?
  Ⓐ between 10 and 15 minutes
  Ⓑ between 15 and 25 minutes
  Ⓒ between 25 and 35 minutes
  Ⓓ between 35 and 45 minutes

10. Bruno unpacked 7 boxes of Frisbees. Each box contained 76 Frisbees. *About* how many Frisbees did Bruno unpack altogether?
  Ⓐ 200
  Ⓑ 300
  Ⓒ 400
  Ⓓ 500

Your time: _____   Number right:_____

On this lesson I did _____ because_____

_____ .

Lesson 4: Decimals and Fractions

Directions Darken the circle by the correct answer to each problem.

Testing Tips

1. Keep the decimal points lined up when you are doing computation.
2. You can add a zero to the end of a decimal number without changing its value.
3. Always put a decimal point in the correct place in your answer.
4. Remember that a fraction stands for a part of a whole amount.
5. Equivalent fractions name the same amount.
6. Divide both terms of a fraction by a common factor to find the simplest form of a fraction.

Sample A:

$$4.68$$
$$+ 2.85$$
$$\rule{3cm}{0.4pt}$$

Ⓐ 7.53
Ⓑ 70.53
Ⓒ 753
Ⓓ 75.30

Answer

The correct answer is *A. 7.53*. The other answers either have the decimal point in the wrong place or do not have a decimal point.

Sample B:

Which is the missing number in this set of equivalent fractions?

$$\frac{3}{4} \times \frac{4}{4} = \frac{\square}{16}$$

Ⓐ 8
Ⓑ 10
Ⓒ 16
Ⓓ 12

Answer

The correct answer is *D. 12*. $\frac{12}{16}$ is equivalent to $\frac{3}{4} \times \frac{4}{4}$.

Now Try These   *You have 25 minutes.*

1. 4.622×100

Ⓐ 462.2
Ⓑ 46.22
Ⓒ 46.022
Ⓓ 4.622

2. Which number sentence is true?

Ⓐ $0.8 < 0.80$
Ⓑ $0.8 = 0.80$
Ⓒ $0.8 > 0.80$
Ⓓ $0.8 = 0.08$

GO ON ⇨

Lesson 4, page 2

3. Which decimal number has a 4 in the tens place, a three in the ones place, and a five in the hundredths place?

- Ⓐ 43.05
- Ⓑ 534.00
- Ⓒ 53.40
- Ⓓ 4.305

4. 15.8 + 3.54 =

- Ⓐ 18.43
- Ⓑ 18.44
- Ⓒ 19.34
- Ⓓ 12.26

5. $16.40
    − 3.98

- Ⓐ $12.42
- Ⓑ $12.52
- Ⓒ $13.42
- Ⓓ $20.38

6. $49.62
    ×   8

- Ⓐ $397.86
- Ⓑ $487.96
- Ⓒ $396.96
- Ⓓ $498.62

7. 23) $7.82

- Ⓐ 34
- Ⓑ $34
- Ⓒ $3.40
- Ⓓ $0.34

8. Ian measured 2.568 inches of rain in September, 2.674 inches of rain in October, 2.439 inches of rain in November, and 2.136 inches of rain in December. During which month did it rain most?

- Ⓐ September
- Ⓑ October
- Ⓒ November
- Ⓓ December

9. Raoul has saved $3.10 to buy a new baseball glove. He needs five times that amount for the glove. How much does the glove cost?

- Ⓐ $5.10
- Ⓑ $51.00
- Ⓒ $15.00
- Ⓓ $15.50

10. What decimal shows the part of this figure that is shaded?

- Ⓐ 0.058
- Ⓑ 0.58
- Ⓒ 0.42
- Ⓓ 5.8

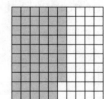

11. What is the sum of 0.89 + 2.361 after each decimal is rounded to the nearest whole number?

- Ⓐ 4
- Ⓑ 1
- Ⓒ 3
- Ⓓ 2

GO ON ⇨

Lesson 4: Decimals and Fractions
Higher Scores on Math Standardized Tests 4, SV 2063-X

Lesson 4, page 3

12. Charlie has $3.00 to spend at the movies. If he buys a drink for $0.78 and popcorn for $1.27, how much money will he have left?

  Ⓐ $2.05

  Ⓑ $0.95

  Ⓒ $1.05

  Ⓓ $0.85

13.
$$\begin{array}{r} 2.32 \\ -\ 0.35 \\ \hline \end{array}$$

  Ⓐ 2.67

  Ⓑ 1.97

  Ⓒ 2.03

  Ⓓ 0.97

14. Which decimal shows how much of this group is shaded?

  Ⓐ 1.9

  Ⓑ 0.01

  Ⓒ 1.01

  Ⓓ 1.1

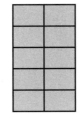

15. What is the lowest term for the answer to $\frac{13}{16} - \frac{5}{16}$?

  Ⓐ $\frac{12}{16}$

  Ⓑ $\frac{1}{2}$

  Ⓒ $\frac{3}{8}$

  Ⓓ $\frac{8}{16}$

16. What fraction of this triangle is shaded?

  Ⓐ $\frac{1}{3}$

  Ⓑ $\frac{1}{4}$

  Ⓒ $\frac{2}{3}$

  Ⓓ $\frac{1}{2}$

17. Find the difference between $4\frac{7}{24}$ and $3\frac{1}{24}$. Reduce the answer to its lowest terms.

  Ⓐ $1\frac{6}{24}$

  Ⓑ $7\frac{8}{24}$

  Ⓒ $1\frac{8}{24}$

  Ⓓ $1\frac{1}{4}$

18. Change $2\frac{2}{3}$ into an improper fraction.

  Ⓐ $\frac{8}{3}$

  Ⓑ $\frac{7}{3}$

  Ⓒ $\frac{5}{2}$

  Ⓓ $\frac{22}{3}$

19. Which shaded part represents the smallest fraction?

  Ⓐ ▢ $= \frac{1}{4}$

  Ⓑ ▢ $= \frac{1}{2}$

  Ⓒ ▢ $= \frac{1}{3}$

  Ⓓ ▢ $= \frac{1}{8}$

GO ON ⇨

Lesson 4: Decimals and Fractions
Higher Scores on Math Standardized Tests 4, SV 2063-X

Lesson 4, page 4

20. Which of these has $\frac{1}{4}$ of its area shaded?

Ⓐ A
Ⓑ B
Ⓒ C
Ⓓ D

    △ ◔ ⊠ ▥
    A   **B**   **C**   **D**

21. Kai's mother made three dozen spring rolls for the school food festival. One fourth of them were eaten by the first group of visitors. How many were still left?

Ⓐ 27
Ⓑ 12
Ⓒ 36
Ⓓ 9

22. $7\frac{3}{20} + 5\frac{7}{20} =$

Ⓐ $12\frac{2}{20}$
Ⓑ $12\frac{1}{2}$
Ⓒ $12\frac{4}{5}$
Ⓓ $12\frac{4}{20}$

23. $\begin{array}{r} \frac{1}{2} \\ -\frac{3}{14} \\ \hline \end{array}$

Ⓐ $\frac{2}{7}$
Ⓑ $\frac{3}{14}$
Ⓒ $\frac{7}{14}$
Ⓓ $\frac{13}{14}$

24. Nina used $\frac{2}{3}$ cup of sugar in her apple muffins. Laurel used $\frac{5}{8}$ cup sugar in her apple muffins. How much more sugar did Nina use?

Ⓐ $\frac{3}{8}$
Ⓑ $\frac{1}{3}$
Ⓒ $\frac{1}{24}$
Ⓓ $\frac{1}{4}$

25. $\frac{2}{5} \times ? = \frac{4}{10}$

Ⓐ $\frac{1}{2}$
Ⓑ $\frac{4}{25}$
Ⓒ $\frac{1}{5}$
Ⓓ $\frac{2}{2}$

26. $\frac{3}{4} \times \frac{5}{5} =$

Ⓐ $\frac{3}{4}$
Ⓑ $\frac{8}{9}$
Ⓒ $\frac{8}{20}$
Ⓓ $\frac{35}{45}$

27. $\frac{1}{8}$ of 320 =

Ⓐ 4
Ⓑ 40
Ⓒ 44
Ⓓ 80

Your time: _____ Number right: _____

On this lesson I did _____ because _____

_____ .

Lesson 5: Measurement

Directions Darken the circle by the correct answer to each problem.

⚡ Testing Tips

1. Study the information given about each measurement before you answer the question.
2. Be sure to choose the correct unit of measurement to solve the problem.
3. Play close attention to the minute and hour hands on the clocks in time problems.

Sample:

Alyssa put some muffins in the oven at the time shown on the clock. They will be ready at 7:05. How many minutes will they take to bake?

Ⓐ 20
Ⓑ 15
Ⓒ 25
Ⓓ 10

Answer

The correct answer is *A. 20*. Alyssa put the muffins in at 6:45. The muffins were done at 7:05. The time between 6:45 and 7:05 is *20* minutes.

⏱ Now Try These *You have 10 minutes.*

1. Which digital display tells about the time on this clock?

Ⓐ 4:29
Ⓑ 6:20
Ⓒ 4:22
Ⓓ 6:35

2. Which unit of measure would you use to describe the weight of a watermelon?
   Ⓐ gram
   Ⓑ liter
   Ⓒ kilogram
   Ⓓ centimeter

3. Which unit of measure describes the length of a letter?
   Ⓐ feet
   Ⓑ inches
   Ⓒ yards
   Ⓓ miles

4. The average person breathes 15 times a minute. How many times does a person breathe in a half hour?
   Ⓐ 30
   Ⓑ 450
   Ⓒ 900
   Ⓓ 45

GO ON ⇨

Lesson 5, page 2

5. What is the temperature on this thermometer?

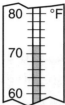

Ⓐ 68°

Ⓑ 72°

Ⓒ 70°

Ⓓ 69°

6. Mrs. Garza offered to make lemonade for the school picnic. She plans to make 20 quarts. How many gallons of lemonade will Mrs. Garza make?

Ⓐ 10 gallons

Ⓑ 5 gallons

Ⓒ 3 gallons

Ⓓ 8 gallons

7. How many inches long is rod C?

Ⓐ $4\frac{1}{2}$ inches

Ⓑ 2 inches

Ⓒ $1\frac{1}{2}$ inches

Ⓓ $3\frac{1}{2}$ inches

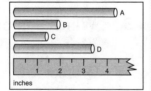

8. What time is it 3 hours after 11:00 A.M.?

Ⓐ 2 P.M.

Ⓑ 2 A.M.

Ⓒ 1 P.M.

Ⓓ 1 A.M.

9. Chelsea needs 24 feet of lace for her costume. The lace is sold by the yard. How many yards of lace will she need?

Ⓐ 9 yards

Ⓑ 10 yards

Ⓒ 8 yards

Ⓓ 6 yards

10. Which unit of measurement is best to use to find out how much a tractor weighs?

Ⓐ ounces

Ⓑ rods

Ⓒ inches

Ⓓ pounds

11. What time will it be in 50 minutes?

Ⓐ 3:00

Ⓑ 3:05

Ⓒ 2:55

Ⓓ 3:10

12. Which of these has a length that is best measured in feet?

Ⓐ a book

Ⓑ a nail

Ⓒ a hamster

Ⓓ a bicycle

Your time: _____ Number right: _____

On this lesson I did _____ because _____

_____ .

Name _____   Date _____

Lesson 6: Geometry

Directions Darken the circle by the correct answer to each problem.

 **Testing Tips**

1. Study the figures and objects pictured before you answer the question.
2. Remember that perimeter is the distance around the outside of a figure, area is the measurement of the inside of a figure, and volume is the number of cubic units in a three-dimensional figure.

Sample:

What is the perimeter of this rectangle?

Ⓐ 49 cm
Ⓑ 10 cm
Ⓒ 14 cm
Ⓓ 4 cm

2 cm

5 cm

Answer

The correct answer is *C. 14 cm.* You find the perimeter of a figure by adding the distances around the outside of the figure.

Now Try These   *You have 25 minutes.*

1. Which of these figures has a right angle?

Ⓐ ∟   Ⓑ ⌃

Ⓒ ⟍   Ⓓ ⋁

2. What is the letter name of a radius in this circle?

Ⓐ XZ
Ⓑ XYZ
Ⓒ ZX
Ⓓ YZ

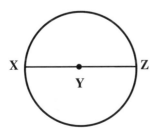

3. Which of these figures shows a line of symmetry?

Ⓐ ▯   Ⓑ ◱

Ⓒ ▯   Ⓓ ▭

4. Which of these is a chord?

Ⓐ AC
Ⓑ CB
Ⓒ AB
Ⓓ CD

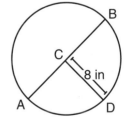

8 in

GO ON ⇨

5. This is a diagram of the playground at Beata's school. What is its perimeter?

Ⓐ 114 m
Ⓑ 105 m
Ⓒ 135 m
Ⓓ 125 m

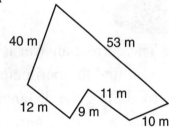

6. Which of these line segments intersect?

Ⓐ AB and EF
Ⓑ AB and GH
Ⓒ CD and GH
Ⓓ EF and GH

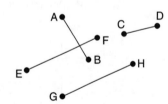

7. What is the name of the figure shown here?

Ⓐ octagon
Ⓑ quadrilateral
Ⓒ hexagon
Ⓓ pentagon

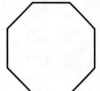

8. What is the area of the shaded section of this figure in square units?

Ⓐ 5
Ⓑ 17
Ⓒ 25
Ⓓ 20

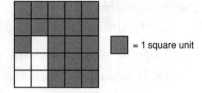

9. Which statement about this drawing is true?

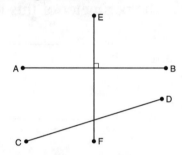

Ⓐ AB is parallel to CD.
Ⓑ AB is perpendicular to EF.
Ⓒ CD is perpendicular to EF.
Ⓓ EF is parallel to AB.

10. Which of the following best represents a pair of congruent figures?

Ⓐ

Ⓑ

Ⓒ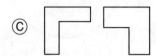

Ⓓ

GO ON ⇨

Lesson 6, page 3

11. Estimate how many of the small shapes are needed to fill the rectangle shown below.

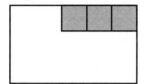

Ⓐ 15
Ⓑ 9
Ⓒ 12
Ⓓ 20

12. Which of these numbered triangles is similar to triangle ABC?

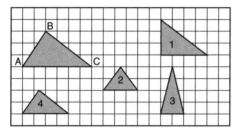

Ⓐ Triangle 1
Ⓑ Triangle 2
Ⓒ Triangle 3
Ⓓ Triangle 4

13. Iris drew a picture of a swimming pool. What is its perimeter in feet?

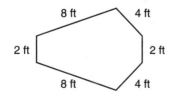

Ⓐ 24
Ⓑ 28
Ⓒ 22
Ⓓ 20

14. Which of these shapes is a hexagon?

Ⓐ   Ⓑ

Ⓒ   Ⓓ

15. How many of the smaller figures are needed to cover the larger figure?

   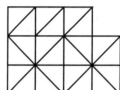

Ⓐ 11
Ⓑ 22
Ⓒ 10
Ⓓ 7

16. Which two figures below are congruent?

1   2   3   4

Ⓐ 1 and 2   Ⓑ 2 and 3
Ⓒ 2 and 4   Ⓓ 1 and 3

GO ON ⇨

Lesson 6, page 4

17. Which of these shows a line of symmetry?

  Ⓐ   Ⓑ   Ⓒ   Ⓓ

18. How many vertices (the plural of vertex) does a rectangle have?

  Ⓐ 3
  Ⓑ 5
  Ⓒ 4
  Ⓓ 2

19. How many angles does this figure have?

  Ⓐ 5 angles
  Ⓑ 8 angles
  Ⓒ 4 angles
  Ⓓ 6 angles

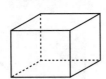

20. What is the volume of this cube?

  Ⓐ 24 cubic ft
  Ⓑ 9 cubic ft
  Ⓒ 14 cubic ft
  Ⓓ 20 cubic ft

21. What kind of angle is this?

  Ⓐ obtuse angle
  Ⓑ acute angle
  Ⓒ right angle
  Ⓓ left angle

22. Which picture shows parallel lines?

Ⓐ   Ⓑ

Ⓒ   Ⓓ

23. What is the perimeter of this figure?

  Ⓐ 16 meters
  Ⓑ 15 meters
  Ⓒ 29 meters
  Ⓓ 25 meters

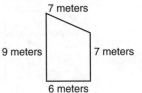

24. What is the area of this rectangle?

  Ⓐ 18 sq cm
  Ⓑ 20 sq cm
  Ⓒ 10 sq cm
  Ⓓ 8 sq cm

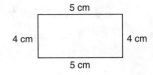

STOP

Your time: _____   Number right: _____

On this lesson I did _____ because _____

_____.

Name _____ Date _____

Lesson 7: Charts and Graphs

Directions Darken the circle by the correct answer to each problem.

⚡ Testing Tips

1. A chart uses columns and rows to show information.
2. A pictograph uses pictures to show information.
3. A bar graph uses bars to show information.
4. A line graph uses lines on a grid to show information.
5. All charts and graphs have a title and a scale to show amounts. They also have categories to tell what information is being shown.
6. First, study the chart or graph carefully. Then, notice the title. Finally, study the scale and use your finger to point to each piece of information.
7. Look for key words or numbers in the question that tell you what to look for in the chart or graph.

Sample:

This graph shows how many students have a dog, cat, both, or neither.

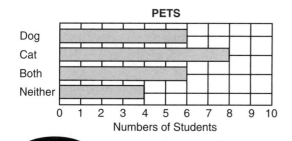

How many students have only a cat as a pet?

- Ⓐ 4 students
- Ⓑ 6 students
- Ⓒ 8 students
- Ⓓ 10 students

Answer The correct answer is *C. 8 students*. There are 8 students who have only a cat as a pet, 6 students who have only a dog, 6 students with a dog and a cat, and 4 students who do not have a dog or a cat as a pet.

⏱ Now Try These *You have 20 minutes.*

Use the chart below to answer questions 1–3.

Area of Largest States	
State	Area (in square miles)
Alaska	591,004
California	158,706
Montana	147,046
New Mexico	121,593
Texas	266,807

1. Which state has an area greater than that of Texas?
   - Ⓐ Alaska
   - Ⓑ Montana
   - Ⓒ New Mexico
   - Ⓓ California

Lesson 7, page 2

2. Which state has about twice the area of New Mexico?
- Ⓐ California
- Ⓑ Texas
- Ⓒ Montana
- Ⓓ Alaska

3. Which state has the smallest area?
- Ⓐ Texas
- Ⓑ Montana
- Ⓒ California
- Ⓓ New Mexico

Use the pictograph to answer questions 4–5.

Musical Instruments Played by Students	
Piano	🎹 🎹 🎹 🎹
French Horn	📯 📯
Trumpet	🎺 🎺 🎺
Guitar	🎸 🎸 🎸 🎸 🎸 🎸 🎸
Drums	🥁 🥁 🥁 🥁 🥁

4. Which is the least popular instrument?
- Ⓐ trumpet
- Ⓑ piano
- Ⓒ French horn
- Ⓓ guitar

5. How many students play drums?
- Ⓐ 4 students
- Ⓑ 5 students
- Ⓒ 2 students
- Ⓓ 3 students

Use the graph below to answer questions 6–8.

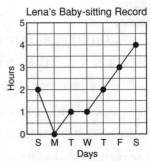

Lena's Baby-sitting Record

6. Lena kept a graph to show how many hours she baby-sat in one week. How many hours did Lena baby-sit for the whole week?
- Ⓐ 10 hours
- Ⓑ 8 hours
- Ⓒ 13 hours
- Ⓓ 15 hours

7. Lena baby-sat for two hours on Sunday. On which other day did she baby-sit the same amount of time?
- Ⓐ Tuesday
- Ⓑ Wednesday
- Ⓒ Thursday
- Ⓓ Saturday

8. How many hours did Lena baby-sit on Monday?
- Ⓐ 1 hour
- Ⓑ 0 hours
- Ⓒ 2 hours
- Ⓓ 5 hours

GO ON ⇨

Name _____ Date _____

Lesson 7, page 3

Ms. Tuft's students wrote stories about a favorite sport they had played recently. The following graph shows the student topics. **Study the graph and use it to answer questions 9–11.**

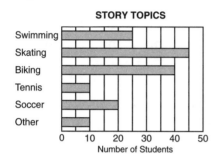

9. How many more students wrote about biking than tennis?
  Ⓐ 10
  Ⓑ 30
  Ⓒ 40
  Ⓓ 50

10. If the students who wrote about swimming had written about skating, how many stories would be about skating?
  Ⓐ 45
  Ⓑ 65
  Ⓒ 70
  Ⓓ 85

11. Which topic did the most students write about?
  Ⓐ soccer
  Ⓑ skating
  Ⓒ biking
  Ⓓ swimming

This chart shows the cost of some lunch items. **Study the chart, and use it to answer questions 12–14.**

Lunch Menu	
pizza	$2.00
hamburger	$1.50
hot dog	$1.00
juice	$0.50
milk	$0.50
fruit	$0.25
chips	$0.50

12. How much would a hamburger, milk, and chips cost?
  Ⓐ $2.50
  Ⓑ $2.75
  Ⓒ $3.00
  Ⓓ $3.25

13. Joaquin has $3.00 to spend for lunch. He wants to buy pizza. What else can be buy?
  Ⓐ milk and fruit
  Ⓑ a hamburger and juice
  Ⓒ a hot dog and chips
  Ⓓ juice and 2 hot dogs

14. Which of the following food combinations costs the least?
  Ⓐ a hamburger, chips, juice, and fruit
  Ⓑ a hot dog, chips, and milk
  Ⓒ a pizza, juice, and fruit
  Ⓓ milk and 2 hot dogs

Your time: _____

Number right: _____

Lesson 8: Probability

Directions Darken the circle by the correct answer to each problem.

 **Testing Tips**

1. Probability is the chance that something will probably happen. The outcome is the result of the activity or event.

2. You can predict the chance that something will happen by using what you observe.

3. When there is more of something in a group or on a spinner, the probability is greater that part will be chosen.

Sample:

On which shape will the arrow stop the most number of times?

Ⓐ pentagon
Ⓑ square
Ⓒ circle
Ⓓ triangle

Answer

The correct answer is *A. pentagon.* The pentagon shape has more space on the spinner, so the chance that the arrow will land on it is greater.

Now Try These *You have 3 minutes.*

1. Brendan is playing a game. If he spins the arrow 5 times, which letter will it probably stop on most often?

Ⓐ A
Ⓑ B
Ⓒ C
Ⓓ D

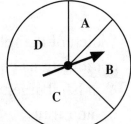

2. Calvin is playing a game using the spinner shown here. If it is spun 7 times, which month do you think it will probably point to least often?

Ⓐ April
Ⓑ May
Ⓒ June
Ⓓ December

STOP

Your time: _____ Number right: _____

On this lesson I did _____ because _____

_____.

38

Lesson 9: Problem-Solving Strategies

Directions Darken the circle by the correct answer to each problem.

 **Testing Tips**

1. Read each problem carefully.
2. Think about the questions being asked.
3. Decide if there are enough facts to solve the problem.
4. Decide the best way to solve it.

Sample:

Mai is planning to ride her bike to her friend's house. She'll ride five blocks east, turn left and ride eight blocks north, then turn right and ride seven more blocks. How many blocks away does Mai's friend live?

Ⓐ make a list
Ⓑ make a table
Ⓒ make a graph
Ⓓ draw a picture

Answer

The correct answer is *D. draw a picture*. Drawing a picture is the best way to organize the information to solve the problem.

🕐 **Now Try These** *You have 25 minutes.*

1. Mr. Richard's class decides to have a newspaper drive for two weeks. The students will work in teams and give a prize to the team that brings in the most paper each week. How can they find out which is the winning team?

Ⓐ make a list
Ⓑ make a graph
Ⓒ find a pattern
Ⓓ draw a picture

2. Chris is going to camp next summer. He will take blue pants, blue shorts, a blue shirt, and a white shirt. What strategy should you use to find how many different ways he can wear the pants, shorts, and shirts?

Ⓐ estimate
Ⓑ find the pattern
Ⓒ make a list
Ⓓ choose the operation

GO ON ⇨

Lesson 9, page 2

3. Mattie's and Angela's ages together are 21. Angela is twice as old as Mattie. How old is Mattie?
   Ⓐ estimate
   Ⓑ choose the operation
   Ⓒ guess and check
   Ⓓ draw a picture

4. Rosita, Inez, and Simon wrote reports about Mars, Jupiter, and Saturn. Rosita did not write about Mars. Simon's planet starts with a *J*. Who wrote about each planet?
   Ⓐ use logic
   Ⓑ choose the operation
   Ⓒ use estimation
   Ⓓ work backwards

5. There are 2 dozen ice-cream pops in the freezer. If 3 children each eat one pop a day, how many days will it take to eat all the pops?
   Ⓐ use logic
   Ⓑ make a table
   Ⓒ find the pattern
   Ⓓ use a multi-step plan

6. Now solve problem 5.
   Ⓐ 8 days
   Ⓑ 1 day
   Ⓒ 4 days
   Ⓓ 2 days

7. A candy shop had 95 large chocolate Santas. It also had 73 small chocolate Santas. All but 10 of the Santas were sold. There were also 56 candy canes. Which information is not needed to find out how many Santas were sold?
   Ⓐ A candy shop had 95 large chocolate Santas.
   Ⓑ It also had 73 small chocolate Santas.
   Ⓒ All but 10 of the Santas were sold.
   Ⓓ There were also 56 candy canes.

8. Each Saturday Trudy earns $1.25 per hour for baby-sitting her little brother. One month she sat for 5 hours each Saturday. There were 4 Saturdays in the month. How much money did she earn?
   Ⓐ choose an operation
   Ⓑ cross out extra information
   Ⓒ use logic
   Ⓓ use a multi-step plan

9. Now solve problem 8.
   Ⓐ $12.50
   Ⓑ $20.00
   Ⓒ $11.25
   Ⓓ $25.00

GO ON ⇨

Lesson 9, page 3

10. The population of Alaska in 1990 was 525,000. What other information do you need to have to determine how this state's population compared to the population of Hawaii?

- Ⓐ the population of Hawaii
- Ⓑ the state with the largest population
- Ⓒ the state with the smallest population
- Ⓓ the population of California

11. Jonah bought a roll of film for $5, a photo album for $8, and batteries for $4. He paid with a $20 bill. If tax is included, what information is not needed to find how much Jonah paid for these items?

- Ⓐ The album cost $8.
- Ⓑ The film cost $5.
- Ⓒ He paid with a $20 bill.
- Ⓓ The batteries cost $4.

12. Hannah swims 25 laps in an hour. Which number sentence shows how to find how many hours it would take Hannah to swim 100 laps?

- Ⓐ $100 \div 25 = \square$
- Ⓑ $25 \times 100 = \square$
- Ⓒ $\square + 100 = 25$
- Ⓓ $25 - \square = 100$

13. Taro has 16 shells in his seashell collection. His brother Shin has 11. Which of these number sentences shows how many more seashells Taro has than Shin?

- Ⓐ $16 + \square = 11$
- Ⓑ $\square \div 11 = 16$
- Ⓒ $11 \times \square = 16$
- Ⓓ $16 - 11 = \square$

14. Bart bought a baseball for $4, a batting glove for $8, and a baseball shirt for $9. He paid for these items with two $20 bills. If the price of each item includes tax, what information is *not* needed to find how much Bart paid for these items?

- Ⓐ He paid with two $20 bills.
- Ⓑ The baseball cost $4.
- Ⓒ The batting glove cost $8.
- Ⓓ The baseball shirt cost $9.

15. The population of Rhode Island in 1990 was 1,005,984. What other information is needed to find how Rhode Island's population compared to Alaska's?

- Ⓐ the area of Alaska
- Ⓑ the area of Rhode Island
- Ⓒ the population of Alaska
- Ⓓ the distance between these states

GO ON ⇨

Lesson 9, page 4

16. Each of Maddy's muffin pans holds 8 muffins. Which number sentence shows how to find the number of muffin pans needed to bake 384 muffins?

Ⓐ $384 - 8 = \square$

Ⓑ $384 \div 8 = \square$

Ⓒ $\square - 384 = 8$

Ⓓ $\square + 8 = 384$

17. A sailboat can hold 6 people at one time. Which number sentence shows how to find the number of boats needed for 168 people to go sailing?

Ⓐ $168 - \square = 8$

Ⓑ $\square + 6 = 168$

Ⓒ $6 \times 168 = \square$

Ⓓ $168 \div 6 = \square$

18. Avram, Monica, and Jan ride the school bus. Avram rides 3 miles more than Monica. Monica rides half as far as Jan. Jan rides 12 miles. How far does Avram ride?

Ⓐ cross out extra information

Ⓑ make a list

Ⓒ look for a pattern

Ⓓ use a multi-step plan

19. The library displayed 8 new videotapes on each shelf of the display case. There are 4 shelves. Which number sentence shows how to find the number of new tapes in the display case?

Ⓐ $8 + \square = 4$

Ⓑ $4 \times 8 = \square$

Ⓒ $4 \div \square = 8$

Ⓓ $8 - 4 = \square$

20. There are 18 girls and 12 boys in Marcela's class. Which of these number sentences shows how many more girls than boys are in Marcela's class?

Ⓐ $12 \div 18 = \square$

Ⓑ $\square + 18 = 12$

Ⓒ $18 - 12 = \square$

Ⓓ $\square \times 12 = 18$

21. For the craft fair, Susan made 38 baby bibs. She made 17 from blue fabric. Which number sentence shows how to find the number of bibs that were not blue?

Ⓐ $38 - 17 = \square$

Ⓑ $38 - \square = 17$

Ⓒ $17 \times \square = 38$

Ⓓ $\square \div 17 = 38$

Your time: _____   Number right: _____

On this lesson I did _____ because _____

_____ .

Lesson 10: Problem Solving

Directions Darken the circle by the correct answer for each problem.

1. Read each problem carefully. Decide which problem-solving strategy to use.
2. Decide if you need to add, subtract, multiply, or divide. Then work the problem on scratch paper.
3. Remember to regroup where necessary.

Sample:

Sandy has $10.00. She wants to buy 2 tapes at the music store. The tapes cost $5.53 each. How much more money does she need to buy both tapes?

Ⓐ $2.00   Ⓑ $1.06
Ⓒ $11.06   Ⓓ $0.60

Answer

The correct answer is *B. $1.06*. To solve the problem, use more than one step. First, add the cost of the two tapes, then subtract $10.00 from the total.

Now Try These *You have 30 minutes.*

1. Mrs. Robinson's class is planning a science fair. They will have 24 exhibits on 4 tables. How many exhibits will they have on each table?
Ⓐ 20 exhibits
Ⓑ 6 exhibits
Ⓒ 28 exhibits
Ⓓ 16 exhibits

2. Lorna has 21 yards of fabric to make a bedspread and curtains. If she uses 4 yards to make curtains and 13 yards for the bedspread, how many yards of fabric will she have left?
Ⓐ 17 yards
Ⓑ 4 yards
Ⓒ 8 yards
Ⓓ 9 yards

3. Sylvia's and Mason's ages together add up to 15. Sylvia is twice as old as Mason. How old is Sylvia? How old is Mason?
Ⓐ 10, 5
Ⓑ 12, 3
Ⓒ 8, 7
Ⓓ 11, 5

4. The Watts family bought a dozen ears of corn for $0.95, 2 pounds of green beans for $0.65 per pound, and 3 gourds for $0.13 each when they visited a vegetable stand. How much did they spend in all?
Ⓐ $2.64
Ⓑ $3.72
Ⓒ $2.98
Ⓓ $1.78

Lesson 10, page 2

5. Stella's dog had 4 litters of puppies. Of these puppies, one litter had 5 puppies and three litters had 6 puppies each. How many puppies did Stella's dog have altogether?

- Ⓐ 23 puppies
- Ⓑ 18 puppies
- Ⓒ 13 puppies
- Ⓓ 10 puppies

6. Omar and Elvin had a total of $4 when they went out for lunch. Omar wanted to buy a hamburger for $1.25, fries for $0.85, and a frosty shake for $0.75. Elvin wanted to buy a hot dog for $0.85, a frosty shake for $0.75, and fries for $0.85. How much more money did they need?

- Ⓐ $0.40
- Ⓑ $0.85
- Ⓒ $1.30
- Ⓓ $2.00

7. Julia had a bowl of cold cereal for breakfast, and Lois had a bowl of oatmeal. The cereal had 150 calories. The oatmeal had 75 calories. How many more calories did Julia have for breakfast than Lois?

- Ⓐ 100 calories
- Ⓑ 40 calories
- Ⓒ 75 calories
- Ⓓ 25 calories

8. At Winthrop Middle School, 748 students will be taking achievement tests in the gymnasium. If the custodians place 34 rows of chairs in the gymnasium, how many students will sit in each row?

- Ⓐ 25 students
- Ⓑ 22 students
- Ⓒ 30 students
- Ⓓ 18 students

9. Dennis bought 4 tapes that cost $2.85, $3.74, $2.94, and $4.35. What was the average cost of each tape?

- Ⓐ $3.47
- Ⓑ $4.23
- Ⓒ $3.15
- Ⓓ $2.98

10. Ian is 61 inches tall. Tomaso is 52 inches tall. How many inches taller is Ian than Tomaso?

- Ⓐ 10 inches
- Ⓑ 2 inches
- Ⓒ 9 inches
- Ⓓ 12 inches

11. There are 30 days in September, November, and June, and 31 days in March. How many days are there in all 4 months?

- Ⓐ 100 days
- Ⓑ 120 days
- Ⓒ 121 days
- Ⓓ 110 days

GO ON ⇨

Lesson 10, page 3

12. Englewood School had a used book drive. They collected enough books to fill 12 cartons. Each carton held 36 books. About how many books did they collect in all?

Ⓐ about 300 books

Ⓑ about 280 books

Ⓒ about 400 books

Ⓓ about 600 books

13. Yvonne works in the school book store. There was a sale on book covers. The sale lasted for 4 weeks. Yvonne sold 122 covers each week. How many covers did she sell?

Ⓐ 488 covers

Ⓑ 400 covers

Ⓒ 800 covers

Ⓓ 428 covers

14. Mr. Collins sold 108 passes last week and 134 passes this week for the riverboat rides. Each pass cost $5.00. How much money did he collect altogether?

Ⓐ $1,210

Ⓑ $1,100

Ⓒ $670

Ⓓ $540

15. The price of a pair of sneakers is between $30 and $40. The sum of the digits in the price is 11. Which of the numbers below could be the price of the sneakers?

Ⓐ $28.01

Ⓑ $33.50

Ⓒ $39.00

Ⓓ $53.30

16. Kevin delivers pizzas for Rose's Pizza House. On Sunday he delivered 9 pizzas. On Monday he delivered 6 pizzas, and on Tuesday he delivered 12 pizzas. How many pizzas did he deliver in the three days?

Ⓐ 15 pizzas

Ⓑ 18 pizzas

Ⓒ 27 pizzas

Ⓓ 21 pizzas

17. There were 18 apples. Six boys shared them equally when they went on a hiking trip. How many apples did each boy eat?

Ⓐ 2

Ⓑ 5

Ⓒ 1

Ⓓ 3

GO ON ⇨

Lesson 10, page 4

18. Mrs. Hunter sold 57 tomatoes from her garden yesterday and another 83 today. If each tomato cost 70¢, how much money did she collect from selling all of them?
- (A) $98
- (B) $100
- (C) $116
- (D) $124

19. Michael bought 2 cookbooks for $7.59 each. If there was no tax, how much change should he receive from $20?
- (A) $4.82
- (B) $4.92
- (C) $5.22
- (D) $5.92

20. The price of a baseball bat is between $10 and $20. The sum of the digits is 19. Which could be the price of the bat?
- (A) $27.91
- (B) $21.79
- (C) $15.95
- (D) $12.97

21. Sam crossed the finish line before Larry. Joe finished behind Sam. Peter beat Sam. Who came in first?
- (A) Sam
- (B) Larry
- (C) Joe
- (D) Peter

22. Donna, Cary, and Brad entered a skating race. In how many different ways could they have come in first, second, and third?
- (A) 12
- (B) 9
- (C) 3
- (D) 6

23. Tony, Andy, and Amy each won a prize in the art show. One won for the best watercolor, one for the best oil painting, and one for the best collage. Andy said, "I like the colors in Tony's watercolor." Amy is a friend of the artist who did the collage. Who did the oil painting?
- (A) Andy
- (B) Amy
- (C) Tony
- (D) a friend

24. Mr. Conti manages a hardware store. He placed an order with a wholesale supply company for 42 cartons of nails. There are 250 nails in each carton. How many nails will Mr. Conti get?
- (A) 10,500 nails
- (B) 1,500 nails
- (C) 5,100 nails
- (D) 50,100 nails

Your time: _____

Number right: _____

Answer Key

Pretest, part 1, pages 3–5
1. C, 2. C, 3. A, 4. D, 5. B, 6. A, 7. C, 8. D,
9. A, 10. C, 11. A, 12. C, 13. A, 14. C, 15. B,
16. A, 17. A, 18. A, 19. A, 20. C

Pretest, part 2, pages 6–8
1. C, 2. A, 3. B, 4. B, 5. B, 6. D, 7. B, 8. A,
9. A, 10. B, 11. C, 12. D, 13. D, 14. C, 15. B,
16. A, 17. C, 18. B

Posttest, part 1, pages 9–11
1. A, 2. C, 3. C, 4. D, 5. A, 6. C, 7. A, 8. C,
9. B, 10. C, 11. C, 12. C, 13. A, 14. B, 15. C,
16. C, 17. D, 18. A, 19. B, 20. C

Posttest, part 2, pages 12–14
1. A, 2. C, 3. B, 4. D, 5. A, 6. B, 7. C, 8. A,
9. D, 10. B, 11. A, 12. A, 13. B, 14. C, 15. B,
16. A, 17. A, 18. D

Lesson 1, pages 15–18
1. B, 2. B, 3. D, 4. C, 5. C, 6. D, 7. D, 8. D,
9. C, 10. D, 11. B, 12. C, 13. D, 14. C, 15. D,
16. A, 17. C, 18. D, 19. A, 20. D, 21. C, 22. B,
23. A, 24. B, 25. B, 26. B, 27. A, 28. D

Lesson 2, pages 19–22
1. C, 2. C, 3. B, 4. D, 5. C, 6. B, 7. A, 8. B,
9. D, 10. C, 11. A, 12. C, 13. A, 14. C, 15. A,
16. C, 17. C, 18. A, 19. C, 20. B, 21. D, 22. A,
23. B, 24. A, 25. C, 26. A, 27. C, 28. A, 29. B,
30. C, 31. C, 32. D

Lesson 3, pages 23–24
1. B, 2. A, 3. C, 4. B, 5. D, 6. D, 7. D, 8. B,
9. C, 10. D

Lesson 4, pages 25–28
1. A, 2. B, 3. A, 4. C, 5. A, 6. C, 7. D, 8. B,
9. D, 10. B, 11. C, 12. B, 13. B, 14. D, 15. B,
16. A, 17. D, 18. A, 19. D, 20. D, 21. A, 22. B,
23. A, 24. C, 25. D, 26. A, 27. B

Lesson 5, pages 29–30
1. B, 2. C, 3. B, 4. B, 5. B, 6. B, 7. C, 8. A,
9. C, 10. D, 11. B, 12. D

Lesson 6, pages 31–34
1. A, 2. D, 3. A, 4. C, 5. C, 6. A, 7. A, 8. D,
9. B, 10. B, 11. A, 12. D, 13. B, 14. B, 15. A,
16. D, 17. B, 18. C, 19. D, 20. A, 21. B, 22. A,
23. C, 24. B

Lesson 7, pages 35–37
1. A, 2. B, 3. D, 4. C, 5. B, 6. C, 7. C, 8. B,
9. B, 10. C, 11. B, 12. A, 13. A, 14. B

Lesson 8, page 38
1. C, 2. B

Lesson 9, pages 39–42
1. B, 2. C, 3. C, 4. A, 5. D, 6. A, 7. D, 8. D,
9. D, 10. A, 11. C, 12. A, 13. D, 14. A, 15. C,
16. B, 17. D, 18. D, 19. B, 20. C, 21. A

Lesson 10, pages 43–46
1. B, 2. B, 3. A, 4. A, 5. A, 6. C, 7. C, 8. B,
9. A, 10. C, 11. C, 12. C, 13. A, 14. A, 15. B,
16. C, 17. D, 18. A, 19. A, 20. D, 21. D, 22. D,
23. B, 24. A

Standarized Test Content Areas
for Grade 4

	CAT/6	CTBS	ITBS	FCAT	SAT (10th ed)	TerraNova	TAKS
Mathematics Computation							
Using Computation	x	x	x	x	x	x	x
(Adding, Subtracting, Multiplying, Dividing)							x
Mathematics Applications and Problem Solving							
Working with Numbers	x	x	x	x	x	x	x
Reading Graphs, Charts, and Tables	x	x	x				
Using Probability and Statistics	x		x	x	x	x	x
Understanding Measurement and Geometry	x	x	x	x	x	x	x
Solving Problems (Including Strategies)	x	x	x	x	x	x	x
Adding Decimals and Fractions	x	x			x		
Subtracting Decimals and Fractions	x	x			x	x	
Using Fractions and Money		x			x		
Using Estimation			x	x	x		

Higher Scores on Math Standardized Tests 4, SV 2063-X